I0461331

COPYRIGHT 2022 © TE'ARA ARMAN
ALL RIGHTS RESERVED. IT IS ILLEGAL TO REPRODUCE, UPLICATE, OR TRANSMIT ANY PART OF THIS DOCUMENT IN EITHER ELECTRONIC MEANS OR IN PRINTED FORMAT. COPYING THIS PUBLICATION IS STRICTLY PROHIBITED AND ANY REPLICATION OF THIS DOCUMENT IS NOT ALLOWED NLESS WITH WRITTEN PERMISSION FROM TE'ARA ARMAN.

WWW.TEARAARMAN.COM
ISBN:979-8-9857625-1-8

Monthly Brain Dump!

Books To Read

Month:

- [ ]
- [ ]
- [ ]
- [ ]
- [ ]
- [ ]
- [ ]

Weekly Tasks

MONTH

WEEK 1

WEEK 2

WEEK 3

WEEK 4

OTHER

NOTES

DAILY WORK

DATE:

TASKS TODAY

FOR TOMORROW

WATER INTAKE

BOOKS TO READ

NOTES

DAILY WORK

DATE:

TASKS TODAY

FOR TOMORROW

WATER INTAKE

BOOKS TO READ

NOTES

DAILY WORK

DATE:

TASKS TODAY

FOR TOMORROW

WATER INTAKE

BOOKS TO READ

NOTES

DAILY WORK

DATE:

TASKS TODAY

FOR TOMORROW

WATER INTAKE

BOOKS TO READ

NOTES

DAILY WORK

DATE:

TASKS TODAY

FOR TOMORROW

WATER INTAKE

BOOKS TO READ

NOTES

DAILY WORK

DATE:

TASKS TODAY

FOR TOMORROW

WATER INTAKE

BOOKS TO READ

NOTES

DAILY WORK

DATE:

TASKS TODAY

FOR TOMORROW

WATER INTAKE

BOOKS TO READ

NOTES

DAILY WORK

DATE:

TASKS TODAY

FOR TOMORROW

WATER INTAKE

BOOKS TO READ

NOTES

DAILY WORK

DATE:

TASKS TODAY

FOR TOMORROW

WATER INTAKE

BOOKS TO READ

NOTES

DAILY WORK

DATE:

TASKS TODAY

FOR TOMORROW

WATER INTAKE

BOOKS TO READ

NOTES

DAILY WORK

DATE:

TASKS TODAY

FOR TOMORROW

WATER INTAKE

BOOKS TO READ

NOTES

DAILY WORK

DATE:

TASKS TODAY

FOR TOMORROW

WATER INTAKE

BOOKS TO READ

NOTES

DAILY WORK

DATE:

TASKS TODAY

FOR TOMORROW

WATER INTAKE

BOOKS TO READ

NOTES

DAILY WORK

DATE:

TASKS TODAY

FOR TOMORROW

WATER INTAKE

BOOKS TO READ

NOTES

DAILY WORK

DATE:

TASKS TODAY

FOR TOMORROW

WATER INTAKE

BOOKS TO READ

NOTES

DAILY WORK

DATE:

TASKS TODAY

FOR TOMORROW

WATER INTAKE

BOOKS TO READ

NOTES

DAILY WORK

DATE:

TASKS TODAY

FOR TOMORROW

WATER INTAKE

BOOKS TO READ

NOTES

DAILY WORK

DATE:

TASKS TODAY

FOR TOMORROW

WATER INTAKE

BOOKS TO READ

NOTES

DAILY WORK

DATE:

TASKS TODAY

FOR TOMORROW

WATER INTAKE

BOOKS TO READ

NOTES

DAILY WORK

DATE:

TASKS TODAY

FOR TOMORROW

WATER INTAKE

BOOKS TO READ

NOTES

DAILY WORK

DATE:

TASKS TODAY

FOR TOMORROW

WATER INTAKE

BOOKS TO READ

NOTES

DAILY WORK

DATE:

TASKS TODAY

FOR TOMORROW

WATER INTAKE

BOOKS TO READ

NOTES

DAILY WORK

DATE:

TASKS TODAY

FOR TOMORROW

WATER INTAKE

BOOKS TO READ

NOTES

DAILY WORK

DATE:

TASKS TODAY

FOR TOMORROW

WATER INTAKE

BOOKS TO READ

NOTES

DAILY WORK

DATE:

TASKS TODAY

FOR TOMORROW

WATER INTAKE

BOOKS TO READ

NOTES

DAILY WORK

DATE:

TASKS TODAY

FOR TOMORROW

WATER INTAKE

BOOKS TO READ

NOTES

DAILY WORK

DATE:

TASKS TODAY

FOR TOMORROW

WATER INTAKE

BOOKS TO READ

NOTES

DAILY WORK

DATE:

TASKS TODAY

FOR TOMORROW

WATER INTAKE

BOOKS TO READ

NOTES

DAILY WORK

DATE:

TASKS TODAY

FOR TOMORROW

WATER INTAKE

BOOKS TO READ

NOTES

DAILY WORK

DATE:

TASKS TODAY

FOR TOMORROW

WATER INTAKE

BOOKS TO READ

NOTES

Monthly Brain Dump!

Books To Read

Month:

- [ ]
- [ ]
- [ ]
- [ ]
- [ ]
- [ ]
- [ ]

Weekly Tasks

MONTH

WEEK 1

WEEK 2

WEEK 3

WEEK 4

OTHER

NOTES

DAILY WORK

DATE:

TASKS TODAY

FOR TOMORROW

WATER INTAKE

BOOKS TO READ

NOTES

DAILY WORK

DATE:

TASKS TODAY

FOR TOMORROW

WATER INTAKE

BOOKS TO READ

NOTES

DAILY WORK

DATE:

TASKS TODAY

FOR TOMORROW

WATER INTAKE

BOOKS TO READ

NOTES

DAILY WORK

DATE:

TASKS TODAY

FOR TOMORROW

WATER INTAKE

BOOKS TO READ

NOTES

DAILY WORK

DATE:

TASKS TODAY

FOR TOMORROW

WATER INTAKE

BOOKS TO READ

NOTES

DAILY WORK

DATE:

TASKS TODAY

FOR TOMORROW

WATER INTAKE

BOOKS TO READ

NOTES

DAILY WORK

DATE:

TASKS TODAY

FOR TOMORROW

WATER INTAKE

BOOKS TO READ

NOTES

DAILY WORK

DATE:

TASKS TODAY

FOR TOMORROW

WATER INTAKE

BOOKS TO READ

NOTES

DAILY WORK

DATE:

TASKS TODAY

FOR TOMORROW

WATER INTAKE

BOOKS TO READ

NOTES

DAILY WORK

DATE:

TASKS TODAY

FOR TOMORROW

WATER INTAKE

BOOKS TO READ

NOTES

DAILY WORK

DATE:

TASKS TODAY

FOR TOMORROW

WATER INTAKE

BOOKS TO READ

NOTES

DAILY WORK

DATE:

TASKS TODAY

FOR TOMORROW

WATER INTAKE

BOOKS TO READ

NOTES

DAILY WORK

DATE:

TASKS TODAY

FOR TOMORROW

WATER INTAKE

BOOKS TO READ

NOTES

DAILY WORK

DATE:

TASKS TODAY

FOR TOMORROW

WATER INTAKE

BOOKS TO READ

NOTES

DAILY WORK

DATE:

TASKS TODAY

FOR TOMORROW

WATER INTAKE

BOOKS TO READ

NOTES

DAILY WORK

DATE:

TASKS TODAY

FOR TOMORROW

WATER INTAKE

BOOKS TO READ

NOTES

DAILY WORK

DATE:

TASKS TODAY

FOR TOMORROW

WATER INTAKE

BOOKS TO READ

NOTES

DAILY WORK

DATE:

TASKS TODAY

FOR TOMORROW

WATER INTAKE

BOOKS TO READ

NOTES

DAILY WORK

DATE:

TASKS TODAY

FOR TOMORROW

WATER INTAKE

BOOKS TO READ

NOTES

DAILY WORK

DATE:

TASKS TODAY

FOR TOMORROW

WATER INTAKE

BOOKS TO READ

NOTES

DAILY WORK

DATE:

TASKS TODAY

FOR TOMORROW

WATER INTAKE

BOOKS TO READ

NOTES

DAILY WORK

DATE:

TASKS TODAY

FOR TOMORROW

WATER INTAKE

BOOKS TO READ

NOTES

DAILY WORK

DATE:

TASKS TODAY

FOR TOMORROW

WATER INTAKE

BOOKS TO READ

NOTES

DAILY WORK

DATE:

TASKS TODAY

FOR TOMORROW

WATER INTAKE

BOOKS TO READ

NOTES

DAILY WORK

DATE:

TASKS TODAY

FOR TOMORROW

WATER INTAKE

BOOKS TO READ

NOTES

DAILY WORK

DATE:

TASKS TODAY

FOR TOMORROW

WATER INTAKE

BOOKS TO READ

NOTES

DAILY WORK

DATE:

TASKS TODAY

FOR TOMORROW

WATER INTAKE

BOOKS TO READ

NOTES

DAILY WORK

DATE:

TASKS TODAY

FOR TOMORROW

WATER INTAKE

BOOKS TO READ

NOTES

DAILY WORK

DATE:

TASKS TODAY

FOR TOMORROW

WATER INTAKE

BOOKS TO READ

NOTES

DAILY WORK

DATE:

TASKS TODAY

FOR TOMORROW

WATER INTAKE

BOOKS TO READ

NOTES

Monthly Brain Dump!

Books To Read

Month:

- [ ]
- [ ]
- [ ]
- [ ]
- [ ]
- [ ]
- [ ]

Weekly Tasks

MONTH

WEEK 1

WEEK 2

WEEK 3

WEEK 4

OTHER

NOTES

DAILY WORK

DATE:

TASKS TODAY

FOR TOMORROW

WATER INTAKE

BOOKS TO READ

NOTES

DAILY WORK

DATE:

TASKS TODAY

FOR TOMORROW

WATER INTAKE

BOOKS TO READ

NOTES

DAILY WORK

DATE:

TASKS TODAY

FOR TOMORROW

WATER INTAKE

BOOKS TO READ

NOTES

DAILY WORK

DATE:

TASKS TODAY

FOR TOMORROW

WATER INTAKE

BOOKS TO READ

NOTES

DAILY WORK

DATE:

TASKS TODAY

FOR TOMORROW

WATER INTAKE

BOOKS TO READ

NOTES

DAILY WORK

DATE:

TASKS TODAY

FOR TOMORROW

WATER INTAKE

BOOKS TO READ

NOTES

DAILY WORK

DATE:

TASKS TODAY

FOR TOMORROW

WATER INTAKE

BOOKS TO READ

NOTES

DAILY WORK

DATE:

TASKS TODAY

FOR TOMORROW

WATER INTAKE

BOOKS TO READ

NOTES

DAILY WORK

DATE:

TASKS TODAY

FOR TOMORROW

WATER INTAKE

BOOKS TO READ

NOTES

DAILY WORK

DATE:

TASKS TODAY

FOR TOMORROW

WATER INTAKE

BOOKS TO READ

NOTES

DAILY WORK

DATE:

TASKS TODAY

FOR TOMORROW

WATER INTAKE

BOOKS TO READ

NOTES

DAILY WORK

DATE:

TASKS TODAY

FOR TOMORROW

WATER INTAKE

BOOKS TO READ

NOTES

DAILY WORK

DATE:

TASKS TODAY

FOR TOMORROW

WATER INTAKE

BOOKS TO READ

NOTES

DAILY WORK

DATE:

TASKS TODAY

FOR TOMORROW

WATER INTAKE

BOOKS TO READ

NOTES

DAILY WORK

DATE:

TASKS TODAY

FOR TOMORROW

WATER INTAKE

BOOKS TO READ

NOTES

DAILY WORK

DATE:

TASKS TODAY

FOR TOMORROW

WATER INTAKE

BOOKS TO READ

NOTES

DAILY WORK

DATE:

TASKS TODAY

FOR TOMORROW

WATER INTAKE

BOOKS TO READ

NOTES

DAILY WORK

DATE:

TASKS TODAY

FOR TOMORROW

WATER INTAKE

BOOKS TO READ

NOTES

DAILY WORK

DATE:

TASKS TODAY

FOR TOMORROW

WATER INTAKE

BOOKS TO READ

NOTES

DAILY WORK

DATE:

TASKS TODAY

FOR TOMORROW

WATER INTAKE

BOOKS TO READ

NOTES

DAILY WORK

DATE:

TASKS TODAY

FOR TOMORROW

WATER INTAKE

BOOKS TO READ

NOTES

DAILY WORK

DATE:

TASKS TODAY

FOR TOMORROW

WATER INTAKE

BOOKS TO READ

NOTES

DAILY WORK

DATE:

TASKS TODAY

FOR TOMORROW

WATER INTAKE

BOOKS TO READ

NOTES

DAILY WORK

DATE:

TASKS TODAY

FOR TOMORROW

WATER INTAKE

BOOKS TO READ

NOTES

DAILY WORK

DATE:

TASKS TODAY

FOR TOMORROW

WATER INTAKE

BOOKS TO READ

NOTES

DAILY WORK

DATE:

TASKS TODAY

FOR TOMORROW

WATER INTAKE

BOOKS TO READ

NOTES

DAILY WORK

DATE:

TASKS TODAY

FOR TOMORROW

WATER INTAKE

BOOKS TO READ

NOTES

DAILY WORK

DATE:

TASKS TODAY

FOR TOMORROW

WATER INTAKE

BOOKS TO READ

NOTES

DAILY WORK

DATE:

TASKS TODAY

FOR TOMORROW

WATER INTAKE

BOOKS TO READ

NOTES

DAILY WORK

DATE:

TASKS TODAY

FOR TOMORROW

WATER INTAKE

BOOKS TO READ

NOTES

www.ingramcontent.com/pod-product-compliance
Lightning Source LLC
Chambersburg PA
CBHW060339130626
46553CB00003B/1053
* 9 7 9 8 9 8 5 7 6 2 5 1 8 *